TO: BRIAN

May God Bless you

G. K. ...

June-19-10

*S*uccessfully *R*aising *Y*oung *B*lack*M*en

Phil-4:13

Successfully Raising Young Black Men

&

Kevin D. Barnes, Sr.

SUCCESSFULLY RAISING YOUNG BLACK MEN

Copyright 2007
TORCH LEGACY PUBLICATIONS, DALLAS, TEXAS;
ATLANTA, GEORGIA; BROOKLYN, NEW YORK

Cover Designed by Bill Hopper of Hopper Graphics

First Printing 2007

The Bible quotations in this volume are from the King James Version of the Bible.

The name TORCH LEGACY PUBLICATIONS and its logo are registered as a trademark in the U.S. patent office.

10-Digit ISBN: 0-9785333-8-0
13-Digit ISBN: 978-0-9785333-8-0

Printed in the United States of America.

To my mother,
Naomi Ruth Barnes,
who has gone home
to be with the Lord.

"Lo, children are an heritage of the Lord:
and the fruit of the womb is his reward.
As arrows are in the hand of a mighty man;
so are children of the youth.
Happy is the man that hath his quiver
full of them: they shall not be ashamed,
but they shall speak
with the enemies in the gate."

—Psalm 127:3-5

Successfully Raising
Young Black Men

CONTENTS

ACKNOWLEDGMENTS

&

First and foremost, I would like to thank my Lord and Savior, Jesus Christ, Who helped bring this book into being. Without Him this book could not have been done.

I thank God for my loving wife, Brenda, for her patience, understanding and unwavering support; and, also, for my sons: Kevin, Keith and Kenneth, whom I love unconditionally. I also wish to thank my brothers and sisters for their influence on my life. I am indebted to my dutiful secretary, Debbie Potter, for her patience in typing the original manuscript; and to the entire Abyssinian Missionary Baptist Church Family, who are some of the best people this side of Heaven. I wish to express my gratitude to my brother and friend, Daniel Whyte III, for his encouragement, inspiration and invaluable assistance and support throughout the writing of this book. Also, I wish to thank the editors of this book, Daniella Whyte and Daniel Whyte IV.

*"If you bungle raising your children,
I don't think whatever else you do well
matters very much."*
—Jacqueline Kennedy

Foreword

Some time back, Pastor Kevin Barnes, of the Abyssinian Baptist Church in Oakland, California, picked up a copy of my book, *Letters to Young Black Men,* from a Walgreens store, near his church. He contacted me and told me he read the book in one setting, with tears in his eyes. Later, he invited me to do a major book-signing in his city. When I met him and his family, I was impressed with the fact that his three sons (two of which are grown) were serving the Lord with alacrity. These young men were not being forced to work in the ministry with their father; they **wanted** to serve in the ministry with their father. This totally blessed my heart, because it is so rare in this day and time, to see grown, young black men who have a loving and warm relationship with their parents and who actually want to serve the Lord.

I said to myself, apparently, Bro. Barnes and Sis. Barnes have done some things right in raising these young men for the glory of God. It is one thing to raise a child, and the child turns out okay, and does not get into trouble. But it is another thing, in this day and time, when you see black parents raise children, who not only turn out okay, but actually are excited about serving the Lord. This is easily said, but not easily done. If it were easy, we would have many more parents today, both black and white, doing it.

After some prayer, I encouraged Pastor Barnes to write this book, not because Pastor Barnes is necessarily a writer, but because Pastor Barnes and Mrs. Barnes have actually raised three young black men successfully. Today, we have many people who write books, but they have not done what they are writing about. Well, Pastor Barnes and his wife have done what they are writing about, and I want you to hear what they have to say and take heed to it.

—Daniel Whyte III
Glasgow, Scotland

"Small boys become big men through the influence of big men who care about small boys."

—Anonymous

Introduction

In August of last year, after reading one of Daniel Whyte's books, *Letters to Young Black Men*, and being greatly impressed by it, I invited him out to our church, Abyssinian Missionary Baptist Church, in Oakland, California, to speak, and to have a book-signing there. After he left California, he called me and told me that he was very impressed with the way my three sons carried themselves when he had been with us, and congratulated me on doing such a good job in raising them. He further went on to share with me, that, in his opinion, a man's greatest success in life is measured by the way his children turn out.

He then suggested that I write a book outlining the principles that I used in raising my sons to help other African-American parents raise their young sons successfully. And this book is the product of that inspiration.

Beyond that inspiration, another reason why this book is in existence, is because I feel as though I am obligated, or indebted, to share the knowledge that God gave me, and that I used in raising my sons, with other African-American parents, so that they can implement this knowledge in their family life.

But, let me say here that this book is not intended for parents whose sons are already grown into manhood, or for parents whose sons are almost grown. Because if we are going to raise our sons up for the glory of God, we have to start when they are young.

In this book, we have included several principles. These principles are not based upon my opinions, or the opinions of anyone else, but, solely upon what the Word of God states. These principles will not work for you unless you live up to them daily, apply them prayerfully, and obey them whole-heartedly.

Stephen Covey, in his book, *Everyday Greatness*, asks this thought-provoking question: *"Will we live our lives in accordance with proven principles, or will we suffer the consequences of not doing so?"* Then, he goes on to describe, quite eloquently, the power of principles:

> *Principles are immovable; they are timeless and*

universal. They do not change. They are no respectors of age, creed, gender, or status—everyone is equally subject to them. Principles provide permanent markers against which people can set their direction in times of both storm and calm, darkness and light.

Thanks to the Einsteins and Newtons of the world, many such principles, or natural laws, have been discovered in scientific domains. Pilots, for example, are governed by the four principles of flight—gravity, lift, thrust, and drag. Farmers must learn to master similar principles, or laws of the harvest. Gymnasts and engineers work within principles of physics, including laws of opposing forces. But neither the pilots nor the farmers nor the gymnasts nor the engineers invented the principles, nor can they alter them. Instead, they can only choose whether or not they will set their courses by them, or suffer the consequences. For while values drive behaviors, principles govern consequences.

If African-American parents grasp the principles contained in this book, and apply them in raising their sons, they will become a part of the solution for the problems that we face in the black community of America.

—Kevin D. Barnes, Sr.
Vallejo, California

"My father didn't tell me how to live; he lived,
and let me watch him do it."
—Clarence B. Kelland

Chapter 1

Parents Need to Have a Strong Relationship with the Lord

"Train up a child in the way he should go, and when he is old, he will not depart from it."
                                                              –Proverbs 22:6

———————

Growing up, I was raised in a very religious home. My mother, who was a single parent, raising thirteen children, of which I am the youngest, made sure that we went to church regularly, and that we grew up in a household of firm believers who loved the Lord. My wife, Brenda, also grew up in a very religious home, and when we first started dating, it seemed to me that she and her siblings had to be in church almost every day of the week. But, strangely, this was one of the things that attracted me to my wife of now twenty-eight years. We both had two things in common: (1) being raised in a home where a love for the church and the fear of the Lord abounded, and, (2) being raised under the watchful eye of strong parents. And these two simple principles are what we started with in raising our three sons.

Being firm with your sons is important, but having a strong relationship with the Lord, as a parent, is even more important because you will find that as

———————

you raise your sons, you cannot do it in your own strength. You will have to employ the strength of the Lord and seek His divine guidance to bring you through the tough times.

Now, having a relationship with the Lord goes much deeper than being raised in a religious home, going to church every Sunday and reciting your prayers every night. You must know God personally. Why? Because God is the Creator of children, and He can give you the wisdom and insight that you need to raise your sons successfully.

So, here is how you can begin a genuinely strong relationship with God:

1. **You need to understand that you are a sinner.** The Bible says in Romans 3:23: *"For all have sinned and come short of the glory of God."* Everyone in this world has sinned. You are not perfect, neither am I, so therefore, we can never be the perfect parents that we may dream of being. Once we understand that fact, we will be able to humble ourselves and receive the help of God in raising our sons.

2. **You need to understand that everyone who dies without Christ will suffer punishment in Hell because of our sins.** The Bible states

in Romans 6:23: *"For the wages of sin is death..."* The penalty for our sins is spiritual and physical death in a place called Hell. Hell is a place of eternal pain and suffering and God does not want us to have to go through that forever.

3. **You need to understand that Jesus is the only Somebody who can save you.** The Bible says in John 14:6, *"I am the way, the truth, and the life: no man cometh unto the Father, but by me."*

Notice what the Bible says in John 3:16: *"For God so loved the world, that He gave His only begotten Son, that whosoever believeth in him should not perish, but have everlasting life."* Some 2000 years ago, God sent His Son, Jesus Christ, down to earth to die, to be buried, and to rise from the dead for the sins of this entire world.

The Bible tells us also in Romans 10:13: *"For whosoever shall call upon the name of the Lord shall be saved."*

If you believe the facts that were laid out above, and you want to trust the Lord Jesus Christ as your Saviour, please pray the following prayer:

Lord Jesus, I realize that I am a sinner in need of a Saviour. I thank You for coming down to earth to die for my sins. I now believe that You are "the Way, the Truth, and the Life." I believe that You died, were buried, and rose by the power of God. I ask You to come into my heart, save my soul and change my life forever. In the name of Jesus Christ I pray. Amen.

Congratulations on letting the Lord Jesus become the center of your life. Now, with prayer and obedience to His Word, He will give you the wisdom, knowledge, and strength, and all of the other tools and resources that you need to successfully raise your sons for His glory, praise, and honour.

PARENTING PRINCIPLES
TO TAKE WITH YOU

◆God is the Heavenly Father. Let Him be your parent and example first.

◆If you are going to raise your sons right, make sure that you have the right relationship with the Lord.

◆Understand that since God gave you the children, He is the main One that can help you raise them successfully.

❧

*"Guiding children to having a Christ-centered life
is really the most important thing
a parent can give them.
After all, it involves their eternal future—
forever and ever and ever."*

—Selected

Chapter 2

Introduce Your Sons
to Jesus Christ

"Seeing that Abraham shall surely become a great and mighty nation, and all the nations of the earth shall be blessed in him? For I know him, that he will command his children and his household after him, and they shall keep the way of the Lord, to do justice and judgment; that the Lord may bring upon Abraham that which he hath spoken of him."
–Genesis 18:18-19

———

I hope that you have prayed the "Sinner's Prayer" and have now become a part of the family of God. Now, as a Christian parent, it is primarily your responsibility to make sure that your sons have a personal relationship with Jesus Christ also. Below are three reasons why you need to introduce your sons to Jesus Christ:

1. Because, sadly, in most Black churches today, **you cannot always depend on the church leaders to present a clear plan of salvation** either in Sunday school, or in morning worship. Consequently, many children go to church and are taught all the facts of the Bible, but are left in confusion about true salvation.

2. **Simply because you are saved, does not automatically make your sons saved.** Many people confuse the statement in Acts 16 about the jailkeeper and his family being saved through the witness of Paul and Silas, to mean that when the

———

jailkeeper got saved, the rest of his family was automatically saved. The fact is that Paul and Silas witnessed to the *whole family* of the jailkeeper, (*"And they* [Paul and Silas] *spake unto him* [the jailkeeper] *the word of the Lord, and to all that were in his house."* — Acts 16:32) and the jailkeeper, and every individual member of his family accepted Christ independently of the rest of the household.

3. If everyone in your house has a personal relationship with Jesus Christ, and is committed to serving Him and obeying His Word, then **family life will not only be more harmonious, but more importantly, your sons will be more inclined to do that which is right, while they are young and as they get older as well.**

But merely introducing your sons to Jesus Christ is not the end of the road. You must also emphasize to them the importance of the following in their lives:

• **Prayer.** Pray with your sons everyday. Let them see you pray. Emphasize to them the importance of staying in touch with God because after you are long gone, Jesus will still be there.

• **Bible Reading.** Read the Bible with your sons, daily. Ask God for wisdom in your understanding of the

Word, so that you can explain it to them, and teach them the importance of obeying It. The Bible commands us as parents, in Deuteronomy 6:6-7: *"And these words, which I command thee this day, shall be in thine heart: And thou shalt teach them diligently unto thy children, and shalt talk of them when thou sittest in thine house, and when thou walkest by the way, and when thou liest down, and when thou risest up."*

• **Church Activities.** This not only provides a great way for your sons to build up their own faith, but it also provides a great way for them to fellowship with other Christians. My sons are very active in our church ministry. Not only are they the musicians for our church, but our eldest son, helps teach in our Young Men for Christ Ministry. Our middle son helps with the younger boys. And our youngest is a student of both ministries.

Parents, if you do this today, and you die tomorrow, you would have given your sons the greatest treasure in the world.

PARENTING PRINCIPLES TO TAKE WITH YOU

◆Introduce your sons to Jesus Christ.

◆Emphasize the importance of prayer, and Bible reading.

◆Get your sons involved in church activities.

&

"Your children need your presence more than your presents."

—Selected

Chapter 3

Be There

*"And, ye fathers, provoke not your children to
wrath:but bring them up in the nurture
and admonition of the Lord."*

–Ephesians 6:4

---

*A*fter my wife and I got married, we moved into a one bedroom apartment. It was the kind of house where if you spun around, you could touch the bedroom, bathroom, and kitchen all at the same time. One night I woke up and looked around, and I began to wonder, "How did I get myself into this?" At that moment, I wanted out. I wanted out by any means necessary—because I was afraid—afraid of the responsibility, afraid of not doing a good enough job, afraid that it just wouldn't work out.

That is the stage that many young parents are acting on today—fear. And, sadly, many African-American parents have succumbed to that spirit of fear, have copped out of their marriages and families, and have become the reason behind the national statistic of 66% of African-American children being raised in one-parent households. [Population Bulletin 47, No. 2, August 1992]

God intended for children to be raised in a home

where both parents are present. He never intended for you to have children together, then to shun your responsibility, by getting a divorce, or a separation, and dragging the children back and forth between two homes.

Once children are born into a marriage, and that marriage becomes a family, the focus changes from him and her to "them"—the children in-between. Just in case you have forgotten, according to *Webster's New International Unabridged Dictionary*, a family is "a father, mother, and their children." When one of the parents leave the family unit, this no longer can be called a family, instead, it is a "broken family." And a broken family is one of the saddest things on God's green earth.

Now, making the mature decision to do the responsible thing and stay with your family, through thick and thin, no matter what, is not going to be the easiest thing to do. In fact, this may involve sacrificing your time, your job, your money, and giving up your pursuit of the finer things in life; but, it is the best decision that you can make for your family and for yourself.

Parents, if you are going to successfully raise your sons, you can't cop out, you can't sit down, you can't give up, and you can't let down your sons. The responsibility falls upon you, me, and every black parent in America and the world-over to stop the deadly cycle of broken homes, broken relationships, broken families, and the broken hearts of our children.

PARENTING PRINCIPLES TO TAKE WITH YOU

◆Make the decision to stay with your family so that you can raise your sons in a two-parent home, no matter what.

◆Be willing to sacrifice what you might want and even your comfort to do what is best for your sons.

◆Be there for your sons when they need nurturing, be there when your sons need admonition, be there when your sons are afraid, be there when your sons need chastisement, be there when your sons need encouragement, be there when your sons fail, be there when your sons succeed. Be There!

"The best thing to spend on your children is your time."

—Louisa Hart

Chapter 4

Spend Quality and "Quantity" Time with Your Sons

"And these words, which I command thee this day, shall be in thine heart: And thou shalt teach them diligently unto thy children, and shalt talk of them when thou sittest in thine house, and when thou walkest by the way, and when thou liest down, and when thou riseth up."

–Deuteronomy 6:6-7

Contrary to the world's views, the most important thing that you can spend your time on is your children. Many parents today have their priorities mixed up. They feel that running to the gym, punching the clock every morning, finding a way to pay off the mortgage on a house that costs more than what they can afford, spending time with their buddies, and running to the mall with their girlfriends, is more important than spending quality and "quantity" time with their children. As one family therapist puts it, these people "multi-task their children."

By "multi-task," we mean, these parents are physically present with their children, but they are mentally detached. For example, your son is telling you about something wonderful that happened to him that day, but, you, instead of focusing totally upon what he is saying, are worried about that business deal you are trying to negotiate, or paying your taxes, or balancing your checkbook, etc., and are only half-listening to your son. When the child realizes that you are not really listening, he will try repeatedly to get your undivided attention, and when he fails to do so, he begins to withdraw from you.

By the way, the reason why I keep putting "quantity" in quotation marks is because I believe many parents use the term "quality time" as an excuse for not wanting to be around their children.

When my family was young, it was hard for me to spend regular amounts of time with my sons every day. We were struggling to stay afloat. I was working two jobs, and my wife was working one, just to make ends meet. But, I always made it a priority to visit my sons, while they were at my mother-in-law's house (where they stayed while we were working) and spend some time with them. I would play with them and take Kevin Jr. out to lunch at McDonalds, because I knew that being young, they needed to see and spend time with their father every day. And during the time I spent with them, I forgot about my job, and whatever else I was going through at the time, and focused on spending quality and quantity time with my sons. This helped my sons and I to develop a good relationship.

You may not need to take them to McDonalds

everyday, but here are some things that will help draw you and your sons closer together:

Communicate with Your Sons. In fact, keep such an open relationship with your sons that they feel comfortable talking to you about anything. Remember, if they can't talk to you, they will talk to somebody else, and you and God are the only people who truly know your sons and can give them the correct advice. Keep the lines of communication open, and never be so busy that your sons feel like they can't come and talk with you at any time.

I remember, Keith, the middle son, shared something with me. He said, "Dad, I don't think I am being treated fairly. Every time Kevin or Kenneth ask for something, it seems like you give it to them, but when I ask you it seems like it is a problem." I knew then that Keith was suffering from what psychologists call, "middle child syndrome." I immediately shared with Keith, "Son, I love you just as much as I do Kevin and Kenneth"; then I went on to share with him that since he was the middle child, he was just more sensitive about that sort of thing. That is what I mean by communicating with your sons—not only talking, but listening.

Make Eye Contact with your Sons. I believe that one of the biggest mistakes that parents make is that they don't make and keep eye contact with their children when they are talking with them. There is no way that you can fully understand what is going on with someone, if you don't have good eye contact with them. When I pick my youngest son, Kenneth, up from school, I always make eye contact with him. For if he knows that daddy is going to have eye contact, he will not want to have a bad report, and he will also know that his father loves him and is concerned about him. **Parents, look your sons in the eye, and make them look you in the eye, when you talk to them.**

My mother, Naomi Ruth Barnes, once said, "If you can't look at another person in the eye, something is not right in the middle." I believe what she meant was that if a person can't look you in the eye, there is a good chance something wrong is going on. As parents, I believe God has given you the discernment to look in your son's eyes, and tell what is going on with them.

Learn their Language. You don't have to talk their language, but you do need to learn it. When my sons say, "Dad, that's bad," "bad" to them does not mean bad—bad to them means good. When

I heard Kevin Jr. tell another young man, "Ha, Ha, a rack." At first, I thought that Kevin, Jr. had learned to hang up his clothes. But later I learned that "a rack" meant a thousand dollars.

Take them Places. Let me encourage you, fathers, to take your sons places—just you and them alone. As my sons were growing up, one of the things that we loved to do together, was to go to the Oakland Raiders football games and Golden State Warriors basketball games. This was not only enjoyable, but it was a great way to bond with my sons.

In closing, remember, there is no substitute for the wonderful times that you spend with your sons that make them feel loved and valued. So, forget about your business deal, pay your taxes tomorrow, and balance the checkbook some other day –because your sons need you now.

PARENTING PRINCIPLES
TO TAKE WITH YOU

◆Spend quality and "quantity" time with your sons.

◆When your sons are talking to you, give them your undivided attention.

◆Communicate clearly and often with your sons.

◆Look your sons in the eye, and make them look you in the eye, when you are talking to them.

◆You don't have to speak their language, but you need to learn their language.

◆Take your sons places with you.

"The parent who is afraid to put his foot down will have children who step on his toes."

—Selected

Chapter 5
Taking Authority

"Honour thy father and thy mother: that thy days may be long upon the land which the Lord thy God giveth thee."

–Exodus 20:12

_____

One Friday night, my youngest son, Kenneth, asked to go to a football game with a friend of his. He went to the game and came home around 9:30 p.m. I was sitting on the couch, and Kenny just walked in, looked at me, but didn't say a word. That bothered me because I was the one taking care of him and he was living under my roof. I just couldn't let him come in my house without speaking to me. So, I waited until Kenny went to sleep, then I went to his room and woke him up. I said, "Son, we have to talk. I didn't like the way you came in the house and didn't speak to me. You are fifteen, and you don't have a job. You eat my food, you sit at my table, and you lay in my bed. The clothes you have on, I bought them. The toothpaste you use, I bought that too. So, since I bought everything you have, I think whenever you come into my house, you ought to speak to me."

Now, you may be saying, why wake him up and tell him that. Well, in order to successfully raise young black men, **you need to let them know that you are**

in charge at all times and that they must respect you, no matter how big they get or how independent they become. I am convinced that many parents are afraid of their own sons. It reminds me of a statement that I heard not too long ago: "Teachers are afraid of the principal; the principal is afraid of the school board; the school board is afraid of the superintendent; the superintendent is afraid of the parents; the parents are afraid of the children; and the children aren't afraid of anyone."

I had to later share with Kenneth that respect is the only way to make it. If you teach your sons respect now, they will not only learn to respect you, but will also learn to respect others who are in a position of authority throughout their lives.

I believe one of the main problems parents have in raising young black men, is that they are afraid to take charge and let their sons know who is in charge and who is suppose to obey. Because many parents are under the impression that the way to make their children love them is to give in to their petty demands, give them everything they want, and never say, "No." But, contrary to popular thinking, raising children with this kind of philosophy in mind actually produces a reverse effect. Your children will grow to despise you if you raise them this way; and, furthermore, they will also turn out spoiled, self-centered, and thinking that the world revolves around them.

But, on the other hand, if you are a firm, but loving parent, always willing to put your foot down, when the time comes for you to do so, your children will grow to love and respect you.

You must also understand that your sons will try you at times. They will test you to see if you really mean what you say. The good news in all of this, is that you can stand whatever tests your sons give you, if you do it God's way and remain in charge.

My oldest son, Kevin, Jr., decided to test me one day. I bought him a car when he was in the 10th grade. Because of this new independence that Kevin had, and because he thought all I cared about was the church (during that time, my industrial supplies company had begun to fail, and I had begun to focus more on the church than anything else), he went through this rebellious stage of thinking that he didn't have to listen to me. One day, Kevin, Jr. decided he wanted to go out and I told him no, because I wanted him to stay in. We got into a heated argument about it, and he stormed out of the house and decided he was going out anyway.

I was furious at him for disobeying me. And, as he

left the house, I got into my car and followed him to his friend's house. Kevin jumped out of the car and dashed into his friend's house, leaving the driver's side open. I parked my car and ran to the house after him. He was afraid, and I was furious. By the time I got to the door, Kevin was already inside. I told him that he needed to come home now, and that the car was in my name and that it was coming home with me. Kevin soon learned that his father was in charge and that he would have to do what I tell him.

Parents First, Friends Later. Many parents make the silly mistake of trying to buy their sons' friendship, rather than focusing on that which is more important, which is earning their respect, and demanding their obedience. If your sons learn to respect and obey you while they are growing up, you will have their friendship for a lifetime after they are grown.

Though we should be training and grooming our sons into men, they must understand that you are the parent now, and that you have the last say in making decisions and settling disputes. When they understand that, they will respect you more and be willing to submit to your leadership.

PARENTING PRINCIPLES
TO TAKE WITH YOU

◆Chastise your children while they are young, don't wait till they get older. Put the fear (reverence) of God, and the fear (reverence) of you in them while they are very young. Then as they grow older, they will respect you.

◆You must take charge as a parent, and let your sons know that you are in charge.

◆Understand that your sons will test you at times.

◆Remember, you are not your sons' friend, you are their parent. If you do a great job parenting, your sons will be your friends when they are grown.

"We worry about what a child will become tomorrow, yet we forget that he is someone today."

—Stacia Tauscher

Chapter 6

Recognize Gifts and Talents in Your Sons

"And so he that had received five talents came and brought other five talents, saying, Lord, thou deliveredst unto me five talents: behold, I have gained beside them five talents more."

—Matthew 25:20

———————

I shall never forget how unfaithful our former musician was. Sometimes he would show up. Sometimes he would show up late. And oftentimes he would not show up at all. Well, I got tired of his unfaithfulness to his task. After some time of putting up with that, I said, "Lord, I need a new musician, one who is faithful to the task." The Lord spoke to me by telling me, all that I needed was in my house. However, I continued searching for a musician elsewhere. But God continued telling me over and over to trust Him, because all I needed was in my house.

Well, one day, I took heed to what I thought God was trying to tell me, and I went to Circuit City, bought a Yamaha keyboard, took it home to my oldest son, and told him, "I bought this for you to learn because Daddy needs your help." Well, Kevin took the keyboard and ran with it. He learned to play and while he was learning, Keith got upset and a little jealous because he didn't have a keyboard like

———————

his brother. So, I went back to Circuit City and bought him a keyboard as well. My youngest son kept banging on the pots and everything that he could bang on, so I figured that I had a drummer in the family, and I went out and bought him a set of drums. It took God to show me the talents that my sons have.

I shared all of that to say this: *Recognize the gifts and talents your sons have, and by all means, help them to develop those gifts and talents for the glory of God.*

You may be wondering, how can I recognize and develop my sons' God-given gifts and talents?

1. **Observe your son's behavior, and the things that he likes to do.** For example, if you see that your son likes to draw, you should encourage him in that area, because he may become the next great artist, or the next great architect.

2. **Pay attention to the school subjects that your son does well in, and the subjects that he likes the most.** If you notice that he does well in English and is excited about that particular subject, there are a variety of fields that he could look at going into as a career—editing, journalism, academic writing, or an English professor, just to name a few.

3. **Remove from your sons' vocabulary the words "I can't." Always tell them "You can."** Tell them they can be anything they want to be. Challenge them, because they are capable of doing a great work while here on earth for the glory of God.

These are all great ways of helping you to recognize the God-given gifts and talents in your sons, but most of all, depend on God's wisdom and insight to determine the gifts and talents of your sons.

PARENTING PRINCIPLES
TO TAKE WITH YOU

◆Listen to God's wisdom and direction regarding the raising of your sons.

◆Observe what your sons like to do most, and what comes natural to them.

◆Find out what subjects your sons excel in at school.

◆Always tell your sons "You can do it. God will help you."

❧

"Whatever they grow up to be, they are still our children, and one of the most important of all the things we can give to them is unconditional love. Not a love that depends on anything at all except that they are our children."

—Rosaleen Dickson

Chapter 7

Show Genuine Love to Your Sons –Hugs will Prevent Thugs

"There is no fear in love; but perfect love casteth out fear: because fear hath torment. He that feareth is not made perfect in love."

–I John 4:18

_____

What is missing in many of the homes where young black men are being raised, is a sense of family. I believe that this is the primary reason why many of our young black men join gangs–they do not feel like they are a part of their biological family; therefore, being a member of a gang, gives them a feeling of being wanted and appreciated in a family-like unit. Contrary to what the world says, young black men still need love and appreciation long after they turn eighteen years of age. You are the only person who can give them this feeling, because no one else will love them the way you can.

Now, you may be asking, how can I show my sons that I love them and help them feel wanted in our family? Well, here are some things that I do:

1. **I always tell my sons "I Love you."** No matter how many times a day Kevin, Keith, Kenneth and I talk, I always end the conversation with "I love you." And they always say back to me,

"Love you, Pops."

2. **I hug my sons regularly.** Growing up, I don't remember getting a lot of hugs, and sometimes I believe that that was what I needed most. I would hug my sons before they went to school, and after they came home from school. Hugging your sons lets them know that you are proud of them and that you love them. Even though two of my sons do not like to be hugged, now that they are grown, I still hug them, sometimes.

3. **I encourage my sons.** My wife and I always encourage our boys to be the best that they can be in everything. We do not use the words "I can't" when talking to our sons. It is always "I can."

4. **I teach my sons the importance of team work.** As I mentioned before, all three of my sons play music, and whenever a Gospel group asks one of my sons to play for them, he will always ask, "Can my brothers play also, because we are in this together?" By teaching your sons this important principle, they will feel more accepted than they would if they did everything individually.

---

5. **I keep in mind that all of my sons are different.** In raising sons, sometimes, we must learn to wait on their individual progress. In each of my sons, their needs are different: Kevin Jr. needs the reassurance that he will be okay; Keith needs to be encouraged; and Kenny needs to feel special. Therefore, with all those different needs, I discovered that they each needed time to grow in their own way.

Remember, the more love and encouragement you give your sons while they are growing up, the more confident and secure they will feel about themselves within your family and when they are grown. Hugs will prevent thugs.

PARENTING PRINCIPLES
TO TAKE WITH YOU

◆ Don't be afraid to tell your sons "I love you."

◆ Don't be ashamed to give your sons a hug. They need it.

◆ Yes, admonish your sons when they are wrong, but whenever they are doing well tell them so. Be a blessing to your sons and encourage them.

◆ Teach your sons the importance of team-work.

◆ Realize that all of your sons are different, and they each need different amounts of time to grow.

"In the final analysis, it is not what you do for your children, but what you have taught them to do for themselves, that will make them successful human beings."

—Ann Landers

Chapter 8

Teach Your Sons the Importance of Education

"For the Lord giveth wisdom: out of his mouth
cometh knowledge and understanding."

–Proverbs 2:6

I strongly believe that in order to successfully raise your sons for the glory of God, we must show them the importance of a good, solid education. Our culture continues to discourage our children, especially our young black boys, by telling them that being smart isn't cool. But we must show them that the opposite is true, and that is, being smart is really cool.

My sons were never straight "A" students. They were average students, but they were good students. Out of all three sons, my youngest son has always had the roughest time in school. It was not because he could not do the work; it was just that he did not want to.

One day, in the sixth grade, his teacher gave me a call. She told me that they were having some problems out of Kenneth at school. I decided to handle this problem a little bit differently. I went to school with Kenneth. I sat in his class with him. I went on recess with him. He was embarrassed. But what really got to him was when I made him hold my hand going to and from class. I told him, "You want to act like a baby; I will treat you like a baby."

I knew the importance of education. Obviously, he did not. But that did not stop me from pushing him, and his brothers, to take school and education seriously. Because of this firmness and perseverance, my two oldest sons have finished high school; Kevin, Jr., graduated from college and Keith attended college. My youngest, Kenneth, is still in high school.

In fact, as I am writing this book, I am currently in college pursuing my Ph.D. in Theology. Along with telling your sons about the importance of getting a good education, there are some things we must show them, and education is one of those things. If they see you learning and growing, they will be more motivated to do the same thing.

Now, here are some of the benefits that you can share with your sons, that come from having a good education:

1. **They will have more confidence in life.**

2. **They will be able to support themselves and their family when they get older.**

3. They will be more knowledgeable about the world in which they live.

4. They will be able to think through tough problems and make good decisions.

5. They will be able to help other people.

6. They will be made into leaders, instead of followers.

It is vital that you show your sons that education is important. Though it may be laborious, it will pay great dividends in the future. As the United Negro College Fund slogan goes, *"The mind is a terrible thing to waste."*

PARENTING PRINCIPLES
TO TAKE WITH YOU

◆Teach your sons the importance of education.

◆Share with them the benefits of a good, solid education.

◆Be an example and continue to expand your mind by learning.

*"Children are not casual guests in our home.
They have been loaned to us temporarily
for the purpose of loving them and instilling
a foundation of values on which their
future lives will be built."*

—Dr. James Dobson

Chapter 9

Help Your Sons
Develop Character

"Finally, brethren, whatsoever things are true, whatsoever things are honest, whatsoever things are just, whatsoever things are pure, whatsoever things are lovely, whatsoever things are of good report; if there be any virtue, and if there be any praise, think on these things."

–Philippians 4:8

———

Abraham Lincoln once said on the subject of character: *"Character is like a tree and reputation like its shadow. The shadow is what we think of it; the tree is the real thing."*

That is so true. If you want your young black men to be successful, you must help them to develop character from the inside out. In order to do that, you must have character yourself. Character is not natural for any of us. Because of our sinful nature, we are prone to do what is easy and that which is easy is oftentimes sinful and destructive.

When my sons were born, I thought, just like many of you, that my sons were the most beautiful, most innocent babies in the world and that they could do no harm to anyone. Though they may look like angels, you must realize that they have a sinful nature, and as they get older, they will begin to do things that are wrong. As you know, you don't have to teach children to lie, but you must teach them to

———

tell the truth. Lying may be easier to do at the moment, but telling the truth is what will carry them in the long run and help them gain the trust of people.

Too many parents are giving reason after reason why they cannot raise their sons to be young men of character, honesty, and integrity. You may even be saying right now, "I came from a broken home." "I didn't have a father growing up, so I can't be a good father to my sons." "No one ever developed in me character, integrity, and the sense to do right when everyone else is doing wrong." Let me tell you something, those are just excuses, and they are not worth anything; because even if you did grow up under tough conditions, there is still a chance for you to be the parent to your sons that your parents may not have been to you.

Character doesn't change with the weather. It stands strong to endure the toughest of times. A person with character will realize that he will make mistakes, but at the same time he will accept the consequences for those mistakes, will apologize, get back up, and keep on going. And every parent wants to instill that kind of character in their sons.

Here are my top five character traits that I have tried to instill in my own sons:

1. **Responsibility.** Contrary to what many parents believe, children, boys in particular, love responsibility—they like to be depended on. You can teach them responsibility by giving them jobs around the house to do, like taking out the trash, and hold them responsible for those jobs—"inspect what you expect."

2. **Honesty.** Teach your sons to never tell a lie, under any circumstances whatsoever. Tell them that when they lie, people will not trust them, but if they always tell the truth, people will trust them and have greater confidence in them.

3. **Humility.** Tell your sons that it is okay to feel good about accomplishing great things, but at the same time, let them know that all they accomplish is by the power of God.

4. **Hard Work.** Hard work has never hurt anyone. In fact, it has only helped people. Tell your sons that the Bible says in II Thessalonians 3:10, *"...That if any would not work, neither should he eat."*

5. **Independence.** Young black men need to learn to think independently of others as they grow up because they will have to make their own decisions when they become adults.

Since our children are going to be adults much longer than they are going to be children we need to train them to that end. You are responsible for instilling in them the character traits that they will need to successfully navigate the troublesome waters of life.

Remember, the way your sons act, reflect the way you have raised them.

PARENTING PRINCIPLES
TO TAKE WITH YOU

◆Be a parent of character and integrity in front of your sons.

◆Show your sons the tremendous benefits of good character, and also show them the awful devastation that a lack of character will bring.

◆Develop the following character traits in your sons: Responsibility, Honesty, Humility, Hard Work, and Independence.

"It's not only children who grow. Parents do too. As much as we watch to see what our children do with their lives, they are watching us to see what we do with ours. I can't just tell my children to reach for the sun. I must reach for the sun myself."
—Joyce Maynard

Chapter 10

Be Real in Front
of Your Sons

"Being confident of this very thing, that he which hath begun a good work in you will perform it until the day of Jesus Christ."

———————

–Philippians 1:6

At the church where I pastor, we have a feeding ministry. At one of our meal sessions, the son of a prominent pastor in our city came to our church to eat. He was hungry and had not taken a shower in days. I knew I had seen him before, but to see him in this condition, I almost did not recognize him. Once I recognized who he was, I told him to come to the front of the line and I gave him all the food he could carry with him. After that, I took him to my office and gave him a change of clothes, soap, toothpaste, deodorant, and a comb. We prayed together and then he left.

After this encounter, it really hit me how that this pastor was so prominent yet in the process of building up his church and his ministry, he had lost his son. My mind rolled back to how I almost lost my sons. The church had become my life. I spent so much time handling church business that I stopped going to the movies with my sons, I stopped going to dinner with them, and I stopped spending time with them. It was then that I realized God gave me my sons for me to raise for His glory, praise, and honor. He also showed me that I had to be there for them in the good times, as well as in the bad times.

After that, I went home, apologized to my sons for this failure, and told them how sorry I was for putting everything before them and neglecting them. They forgave me. At first, I thought that we wouldn't be able to put things back together, but I remembered that even if we can't put things back together, Jesus can. I immediately started spending more time with my sons again.

In raising your sons, **you must be honest and real before them.** It is okay to let your sons know that you, too, have issues or weaknesses. Sometimes they want to hear it, sometimes they won't, but, whatever the case, believe it or not, your sons will not look down upon you for making mistakes. In fact, when your sons see you acknowledge your mistakes and failures and apologize for them, they will look up to you more and will feel more free to tell you about their mistakes and failures as well.

Don't be afraid to let your sons see you cry. Some parents think that crying in front of their children suggests weakness. That is not true. Crying can actually bring you closer together. Trust me, when your sons see you cry they will know that you, too, are human.

Don't be a hypocrite in front of your sons. What I mean by this is, don't act one way at home in front of your sons and then act another way in front of other people. Many parents are not consistent in disciplining their sons. By that I mean, they let their sons get away with things at home, yet, when the sons do the same thing in public, the parents look all surprised and some even say, "I have never seen him do that before." Some parents even try to verbally discipline the child. But the child does not obey, because he knows that you are being a hypocrite—that is, you let him get away with these same activities at home, yet in public you act as though you are surprised at what he is doing.

Parents, it is very important that we speak and act honestly in front of our sons. Because, whether we think so or not, our sons are watching us and in the future, they will realize that what you were doing was wrong, then, they will not want to have anything to do with you. At that point there is nothing you can do to remedy it. So, Keep it Real!

PARENTING PRINCIPLES
TO TAKE WITH YOU

◆Be honest and real with your sons. Tell them the mistakes you made, and help them to avoid making those same mistakes.

◆It is okay to let your sons see you cry. It is not weakness, but it shows them that you are human too.

◆Don't be a hypocrite in front of your sons. If you let them get away with wrong actions at home, don't be surprised if they do those same wrong actions in public. Be Consistent!

*"Too many parents make life hard
for their children by trying, too zealously,
to make it easy for them."*

—Goethe

Chapter 11

Expose Your Sons to Real Life (Without them Actually Having to Experience it)

"For I have learned in whatsoever state I am, therewith to be content."

−Philippians 4:11

Many children today grow up with a one-sided view of life. They think that the whole world is just like the environment and the people that surrounded them while they were growing up, therefore, they experience a cultural shock when they have become grown and go out into the real world, unable to function properly as adults.

In order for your sons to live a well-balanced life, it would be wise for you to show them both sides of the track. I remember mentoring a young kid that grew up in a bad part of town. I would go to his part of town, pick him up, and drive around to the other side of town, which, quite frankly, was much nicer. This kid was amazed at the other side of Oakland where he had never been before. It was then that I made up my mind to show my sons the other side of the tracks.

Now, you may be the kind of parent that is very protective of your sons, and so, you may not see the need to reveal to your sons how other people live or the consequences of mistakes that other people make. You may not feel the need to tell them about sin and the bad things of life (i.e. murder, gangs, drugs, etc) because you are trying to raise them in the "perfect home." I understand where you are coming from, but, the reality is, we live in a wicked world, and you need to prepare your sons to avoid Satan's traps.

Now, as you decide to expose your sons to real life, you must tell them why people do the things they do and tell them when someone is doing wrong. If you do so, your sons will grow up more well-rounded compared to the child who is protected from these things all of his life and then is thrown out into the world after he graduates from high school.

As you expose your sons to real life, make sure you do it in a controlled setting. In other words, do not send them out to investigate the world by themselves. Go with them and explain to them that everyone does not necessarily live the way they do.

Another way you can safely expose your sons to real life is through watching selected news, documentary, and fact-based programs on television. If and when you watch television with your sons, when something comes across the screen that may be disturbing to you or your sons or that is different from the life that you live, take the time to explain why people are the way they are and why they do the things they do. Tell them also about the consequences of sin and wrong behavior.

Also, teach them that no one, be they black or white, is better than they are and that they are not better than anyone else. The reason why this is important is because it will help your sons grow up feeling more secure and confident about themselves, and comfortable in dealing with other people, even those who may be different from them.

So, parents, expose your sons to the real world in a controlled environment, so that when they have to face the real world, they will feel secure, balanced, and confident in dealing with other people.

PARENTING PRINCIPLES
TO TAKE WITH YOU

◆ Don't be afraid to expose your sons to the real world.

◆ When exposing your sons to the real world, always do it in a controlled setting.

◆ If and when you watch TV, watch it with your sons, and explain things to them as they come up. A great alternative to the TV is the daily newspaper or the weekly news magazine.

◆ Make sure your sons know that no one is better than they are, and they are no better than anyone else.

"Each day of our lives, we make deposits in the memory banks of our children."
                                        -Charles Swindoll

Chapter 12

What the Bible Says
About Parenting

*"Obey them that have the rule over you, and
submit yourselves: for they watch for your souls,
as they that must give account, that they may
do it with joy, and not with grief: for that is
unprofitable for you."*

–Hebrews 13:17

———————

*M*y wife and I raised our sons with the fear of
God and the fear of the belt. I strongly believe
that there is a lot of truth to the old saying: "Spare
the rod and spoil the child." You can pray for your
sons to act right and you can cry out to God day in
and day out to help your sons to do what is right,
but you had better back up those prayers with the
rod of correction, if you truly want to successfully
raise your sons.

Below are some verses from the Word of God that
will help you exercise your God-given authority in
the raising of your sons:

1. Proverbs 22:6: *"Train up a child in the way he
   should go: and when he is old, he will not
   depart from it."*

2. Proverbs 22:15: *"Foolishness is bound in the
   heart of a child; but the rod of correction shall
   drive it far from him."*

———————

3. Proverbs 23:13-14: *"Withhold not correction from the child: for if thou beatest him with the rod, he shall not die. Thou shalt beat him with the rod, and shalt deliver his soul from hell."*

4. Proverbs 19:18: *"Chasten thy son while there is hope, and let not thy soul spare for his crying."*

5. Proverbs 29:15: *"The rod and reproof give wisdom: but a child left to himself bringeth his mother to shame."*

6. Proverbs 29:17: *"Correct thy son, and he shall give thee rest; yea, he shall give delight unto thy soul."*

7. Ephesians 6:4: *"And, ye fathers, provoke not your children to wrath, but bring them up in the nurture and admonition of the Lord."*

Contrary to what the world will tell you, chastising your child is not only biblical, but if it is done in love and with the right spirit, it proves to your sons that you love them so much that you will not allow them to do evil and mess up their lives.

Share with your sons daily the following two verses

from the Word of God, for they too, have a responsibility and a command by God as well, and that is, to obey you—their parents:

1. Ephesians 6:1-3: *"Children, obey your parents in the Lord: for this is right. Honour thy father and mother; which is the first commandment with promise; That it may be well with thee, and thou mayest live long on the earth."*

2. Colossians 3:20: *"Children, obey your parents in all things: for this is well pleasing unto the Lord."*

As their parent, you must make them obey the Word of God by obeying you. Make the commitment to God that Joshua made in Joshua 24:15 and that is: *"...As for me and my house, we will serve the Lord."* If you chastise them and teach them from a young age, then you will have less trouble out of them as they grow older.

To successfully raise your sons, you must obey and apply the Bible verses laid out above. You will be blessed as your sons grow up in the way of the Lord, and you will not regret that you did it God's way.

PARENTING PRINCIPLES
TO TAKE WITH YOU

◆For your sons to turn out right, you must obey Biblical principals in raising your sons.

◆When your sons disobey you, do not be afraid to chastise them.

◆Make your sons obey you by obeying the Word of God, which tells them to be obedient to you as a parent.

&

"A mother's example sketches the outline of her child's character."

—H. O. Ward

Chapter 13

From Mother to Mother

by Mrs. Brenda Barnes

"The aged women likewise, that they be in behaviour as becometh holiness, not false accusers, not give to much wine, teachers of good things; That they may teach the young women to be sober, to love their husbands, to love their children, To be discreet, chaste, keepers at home, good, obedient to their own husbands, that the word of God be not blasphemed."

–Titus 2:3-5

---

*E*ven though many parents believe it is solely the father's responsibility to train the children, especially the sons, mothers also have a responsibility in that area as well. A mother's disciplining of her children is a part of the father's training. There is a saying that goes like this: "The wife is the spiritual candle of the home." That is so true. If we do our part as the wife and mother, it makes not only our job easier, but it also makes our husband's job easier, and it sets a more peaceful tone for the entire family, especially for our children.

Below are some basic principles that if we prayerfully do, will help point our sons in the right way:

1. **Obey your husband in all things, including the raising of your sons.** If you are obedient to your husband, your sons will be more inclined, not only to obey their father, but to obey you also. Whatever method of chastisement your husband chooses to use

on your sons, stand with him on that. Never take sides with your sons against their father because this will lead to your sons eventually disobeying their father, thinking that you will always take up for them. This will create problems for you as well. Let them see you and your husband as one.

2. **Respect your husband at all times and especially in front of your sons**. Always talk respectfully of your husband and to your husband, and always carry on in his absence, as though he were physically there. I remember there were many times when my husband had to travel out-of-town by himself. It was during these absences that I had to decide whether or not to chastise my sons whenever they did wrong so that they wouldn't grow up believing that simply because daddy is not around, I have freedom to do as I please. Carrying out the disciplining of your sons in their father's absence will teach them to respect you also.

3. **Begin chastising your children from an early age.** As mothers, we tend to have a softer heart for our children and there is the tendency to let them get away with many things. If you chastise them and teach them while they are young, you will have fewer troubles out of them as they grow older. I thank God I have a husband who did not "spare for my sons' crying." He stood firm on applying the Bible verse: *"And, ye fathers, bring them up in the nurture and*

admonition of the Lord."

4. **Love your children**. Contrary to what many believe, loving your children is not letting them get away with disobedience. Love is also spending quality as well as "quantity" time with your sons. I decided to quit my job and work at home (the Lord allowed me to open up my own day care at home), so that I could stay with my sons. When they were very young, I often had to set aside washing and house cleaning so that I could crawl around on the floor with them. I will never forget those days. I had to set aside my schedule in the evenings, so that I could spend the time needed to help them with their homework, often times calling their teacher or a family member to explain to me their school work so that I could more effectively explain it to my sons.

Raising three boys was not easy at times. It's not many that have been blessed to have three sons to raise for the glory of God. I am not saying my boys are perfect, but what I would like to say here to Kevin Jr., Keith, and Kenneth is, Mama loves you very much. Also, to my husband Kevin, you have fulfilled every dream in my life. You have made sure your sons nor I ever wanted for anything, and as I always tell you, I love you more today than yesterday.

Love and Hope for Single Mothers

Just in case you are a single mother raising a son, you can, with God's help, raise them right. The Bible is God's guideline for the nurturing and training of your sons. Prayerfully ask the Lord for wisdom and strength in training your sons, and prayerfully apply the principles laid out in the Word of God.

One of my favorite verses is Philippians 4:13, *"I can do all things through Christ which strengtheneth me."* This verse has carried me through many tough times in my life, as well as through raising and training my sons, and it will you too.

Now, I thank God that I have been able to raise my sons with the benefit of a husband, who has been there for his sons and who took the lead in raising our sons. But, I know that there are thousands of single mothers out there, who are raising their sons without the benefit of a husband. I want to encourage you by saying this: it can be done. Many before you have done it, and you can do it with God's help. Here is what Dr. James Dobson said in his popular book, *Bringing Up Boys:*

> "To every single mom who is on this quest, let me emphasize first that you have an invaluable resource in our heavenly Father. He created your children and they are precious to Him. How do I know that? Because He said repeatedly in His

Word that He has a special tenderness for fatherless children and their mothers. There are many references in Scripture to their plight. For example:

> *"For the Lord your God is God of gods, and Lord of lords, a great God, a mighty, and a terrible,which regardeth not persons, nor taketh reward: He doeth execute the judgement of the fatherless and widow."* (Deuteronomy 10:17-18)

> *"Cursed be he that perverteth the judgement of the stranger, fatherless, and widow. And all the people shall say, Amen."* (Deuteronomy 27:19)

> *"A father of the fatherless, and a judge of the widows, is God in his holy habitation."* (Psalm 68:5)

> *"And oppress not the widow, nor the fatherless, the stranger, nor the poor; and let none of you imagine evil against his brother in your heart."* (Zechariah 7:10)

The message is very clear, isn't it? The Lord is watching over the oppressed, the poor, the downtrodden, and the child who has no father. And yes, He is concerned about your children too. He is waiting for you to ask Him for help. I have seen miraculous answers to prayer on behalf of those who have sought His help in what seemed like impossible situations."

May the Lord bless you as you strive to raise your sons for His glory, praise and honour.

*"Children are our most valuable resource
for the future."*
—John F. Kennedy

Chapter 14

Sons Honour
their Parents

*"Honour thy father and thy mother:
that thy days may be long upon
the land which the Lord thy God giveth thee."*

–Exodus 20:12

---

from Kevin Darnell Barnes, Jr.

When I was asked to write this, I didn't know what I would say, because I am not a good writer. But when asked what my parents mean to me, there were plenty of things that crossed my mind; I just couldn't put it into words. However, what I can say from my heart is, my parents are caring, sharing, helping, loving, and most importantly, they are my heroes. Even today, I say that I want to be just like them. They always tell me that they are proud of me. Now, it is my turn to let them know how proud I am of them, and there is nothing in the world that I wouldn't do for them. Pops and Mom, I love you, keep up the good work, and always remember you are my heroes.

from Keith Dwayne Barnes

I've watched my parents ever since I was a child, and they have both proved to be great role-models. And even though I am not living at home anymore, one of the things that I appreciate the most is that I can call them for any kind of help. When I get married and have children, I want to be the father to my children that my father is to me. I am very blessed to have parents who were there for me every day since I was born. I have never had to wonder where they were, because they have always been there. Love you Pops and Mom!

from Kenneth Dwight Barnes

My parents are good and understanding. They teach me right from wrong. They are nice, caring, loving and giving. I think both of my parents are special. Thanks Pops and Mom!

Chapter 15
20 Key Things You Must Teach Your Sons

"Young men likewise exhort to be sober minded. In all things shewing thyself a pattern of good works: in doctrine shewing uncorruptness, gravity, sincerity, Sound speech, that cannot be condemned; that he that is of the contrary part may be ashamed, having no evil thing to say of you."

–Titus 2:6-8

_____

*B*elow are some things that I believe every young black man needs to be taught while growing up into full-grown manhood.

1. God needs to be first in their lives.

2. To honor their father and mother.

3. How to get a hold of God through prayer.

4. How to get strengthened through reading the Word of God.

5. How to obey the Word of God and live under the blessings of God.

6. That sex before marriage is out of the will of God for men as well as for women.

7. That homosexuality is an abomination in the sight of God and should never be considered.

_____

According to Dr. James Dobson's book, *Bringing Up Boys*, homosexuality is not genetically transmitted as some false teachers say. "If homosexuality were genetically transmitted, it would be inevitable, immutable, irrestible, and untreatable. Fortunately, it is not. Prevention is effective. Change is possible. Hope is available. And Christ is in the business of healing." God made men to be attracted to women. He never intended for men to be attracted to other men.

8. That they must study hard and get a good education.

9. That they must work hard to do well in this life.

10. That they are loved by God and you.

11. That they must learn to handle money well.

12. That they are not inferior to men of other races, and that they matter just as much to God as any other man.

13. That they may rise to the top without character, but they will not stay there.

14. To tell the truth and never lie.

15. That the woman he chooses to marry should be a blessing to him and not a cursing, and that he should be committed to that one women.

16. That he cannot have all the beautiful women of the world—only one.

17. To think for himself and to be a leader and not a follower.

18. That time is not to be wasted.

19. How to behave in any given situation. They need to be taught about etiquette and protocol.

20. That he must have a God-given passion to live for, work for, and if necessary die for.

RESOURCES TO HELP RAISE YOUR SONS SUCCESSFULLY

1. *Bringing Up Boys,* by James Dobson

2. *A Man's Role in the Home,* by Tony Evans

3. *No More Excuses: Be the Man God Wants You to Be,* by Tony Evans

4. *So You Call Yourself A Man,* by T.D. Jakes

5. *What the Bible says about...Child Training,* by J. Richard Fugate

6. *Letters to Young Black Men,* by Daniel Whyte III

7. *Letters to Young Black Men Study Guide & Leaders Guide,* by Daniel Whyte III

8. *Can I Call You Soldier?* by Harold Davis

9. *MO' Letters to Young Black Men,* by Daniel Whyte III

10. *7 Things Young Black Men do to Mess Up Their Lives,* by Daniel Whyte III

3260746

Made in the USA